HERE COMES SNOOPY

Selected Cartoons from
Snoopy, Vol. 1
by CHARLES M. SCHULZ

FAWCETT CREST • NEW YORK

HERE COMES SNOOPY

This book, prepared especially for Fawcett Crest Books, CBS Educational and Professional Publishing, a division of CBS Inc., comprises the first half of SNOOPY, and is reprinted by arrangement with Holt, Rinehart and Winston, Inc.

ISBN: 0-449-23947-0

Printed in the United States of America

67   66   65   64   63   62   61   60   59   58

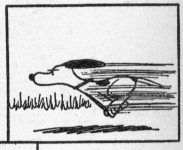

CLUMP!

YIPE!

REAL ALLIGATORS DON'T BITE THEIR OWN TONGUES...

EMPTY WATER DISH!

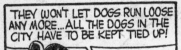

PTUI!

SCHULZ

POW!!

ZOOM!

NOW, YOU CUT THAT OUT!

SCHULZ

BRRRR... THAT GIVES ME THE CHILLS!

I JUST CAN'T STAND TO SEE ANYTHING ON A LEASH!

KLUNK! BUMP!BUMP!
bumpety-bump CRASH!!

WHAT IN THE WORLD WAS **THAT**?!

I GUESS IT WAS SNOOPY..IF HE DOESN'T LIKE HIS SUPPER, HE JUST PUSHES IT DOWNSTAIRS!

SCHULZ

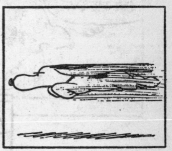

ZIP!

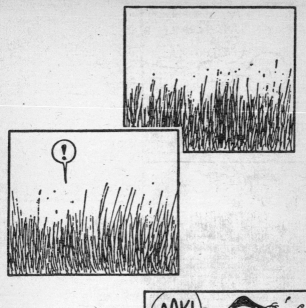

I THOUGHT I TOLD YOU TO STOP THAT DANCING?! YOU HAVE NO RIGHT TO BE SO HAPPY!!! NOW, STOP IT! DO YOU HEAR ME?!

SCHULZ